How to use thes̶e̶ ̶̶̶e̶s

Guided Rea̶

Walkthrough/B̶

A *walkthrough*, or book introduc̶ ̶̶̶̶̶̶̶̶̶̶̶̶̶ ̶̶̶̶̶̶k to a group of children. During the walkthrough, ̶̶̶̶̶̶̶̶̶̶̶ ̶̶̶ to some of the ideas and significant vocabulary they will m̶̶̶ ̶̶̶̶y read the book.

Go through the whole of the walkthrough before the children start reading independently. The walkthrough notes on pages 2 and 3 of this booklet provide prompts for you to use, specific to *How Big Is It?* The questions, comments and suggestions alert children to ideas and vocabulary they will need in order to read independently and with full understanding.

Independent Reading (pages 4–5)

After doing a walkthrough, ask the children to read the text aloud, on their own, at their own pace. Observe the strategies each child uses, praising successful problem solving and expressive reading. Prompts are suggested for good phrasing, use of word-solving skills, predicting and checking the meaning, and actively monitoring the implications of the text, on pages 4 and 5.

After Independent Reading/ Returning to the text (page 6)

After the children have read the book independently, return to the text as a group to reinforce teaching points and to check children's understanding. On page 6, there are quick follow-up ideas for related text, sentence and word level work.

Responding to the text (pages 6–8)

It is important to encourage children to give a personal response to the text. Discussion ideas related to the book are on page 6.

These Teaching Notes also contain group activity ideas on page 7, and a Photocopy Master on page 8, for use after the guided reading session or in a follow-up literacy session.

Guided Reading Notes

Walkthrough

Give a brief introduction to the story to set the context, but leave most of the detail for the children to discover during independent reading.

Cover

PROMPTS (Ask children to read the title and the back cover blurb.) Where are Kate and Joe trying to measure something?

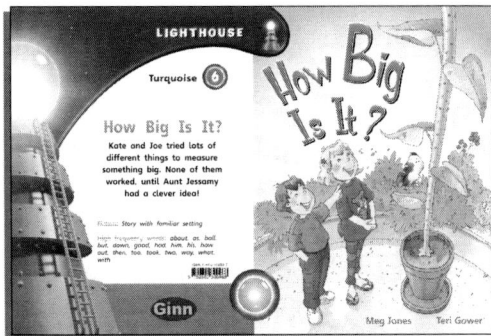

Pages 2–3

PROMPTS What do you think the children are trying to measure? Can you suggest ways of measuring things? Where is the word *measure* in the text? Look for the first letter.

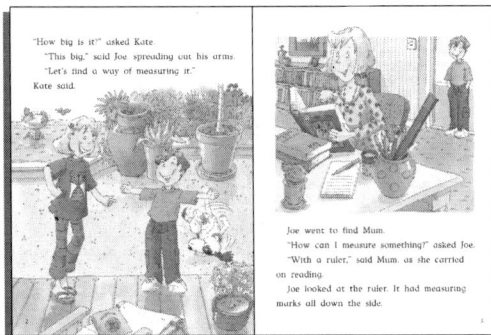

Pages 4–5

PROMPTS What has Mum suggested Joe could use? What do you think Grandma is going to suggest?

Walk on through to page 8, making sure the children have noticed the measuring tools that the various characters suggest.

Pages 8–9

PROMPTS Who's this coming round the corner? She's Aunt Jessamy. Can you find her name in the text? Can you find the dog's name? What helped you to find their names? (Prompt for *capital letters*.)

Finish the walkthrough at this point, so that the children can discover the surprise for themselves. Ask children to go back to the start of the book and read independently.

Pages 2–3

CHECK for *spreading*.

"The *ea* in this word makes an *e* sound as in *bed*. Look at the word ending. Blend the first three letters and sound through the rest of the word."

CHECK for *measuring*.

"Split the word into syllables (*meas/ur/ing*), apply knowledge of phoneme *ea* and blend through the word."

Pages 4–5

something
"Split the word
two and look f
known words w
the word."

CHECK for *answered*.

"Say the first part of the word (*ans*) and think what might make sense. Reread from the start of the sentence to check that it makes sense. The speech marks show that this must be a speech verb."

Ask the child to read on, checking that he or she is reading for sense, and using the grammar for support.

Pages 10–11

Kate and Joe liked Aunt Jessamy. She was always good fun.
She jumped in front of Frazzle and stopped him in his tracks. He dropped the wool. He looked very pleased with himself as he wagged his tail.
Aunt Jessamy chuckled. "You rascal!" she smiled, patting Frazzle on the head.

Then she saw Joe and Kate standing by her side.
"What are you two doing here?" she asked.
"We are trying to measure this," they said, "but it's too big for us."

CHECK for awareness of grammatical agreement in *stopped him in his tracks*. "What has Aunt Jessamy done to Frazzle?" Prompt for *made him stop*. "Look at the words *him* and *his*. Who has stopped?"

Pages 12–13

"What about measuring it with my ball of wool?" she said. Aunt Jessamy always had an answer for everything.
Joe and Kate had never heard of measuring things with a ball of wool. They thought about how they could do it.

"I'll bend it down, and you hold the wool against it," Aunt Jessamy said.
Joe held the end and Kate unrolled the ball of wool. When she reached the top, Kate broke off the wool.

CHECK the child's prediction for what Joe and Kate want to measure.

CHECK that the child follows what is happening, looking at text and illustrations.

Ask the child to read on, using the punctuation to follow the speech.

Page 16

CHECK that the child uses the speech verbs and exclamation marks to read with expression.

Frazzle got so excited by all the noise that he ran away with Aunt Jessamy's ball of wool.
"Stop!" everyone called to Frazzle. But it was too late. He had wrapped the wool all round Aunt Jessamy!

5

After Independent Reading/Returning to the text

Word knowledge – use word endings to support reading

Read the page again and find words with *ed* endings, e.g. *asked*, *mumbled*, *pointed* and *propped*. Ensure the children are clear that *ed* endings on verbs indicate past tense. Write up some present tense versions of regular verbs used in the text, such as *stretch*, *measure*, *carry*, *show*, *point* and *chuckle*. Ask children to write the past tense version of each verb. Discuss spelling rules, e.g. changing *y* to *i*.

Sentence knowledge – use words and phrases to link sentences

Write examples of words that link sentences on the flipchart. For example, *first*, *then*, *next*, *but*, *after a while* and *meanwhile*. Ask the children to retell the story using some of the words on the flipchart.

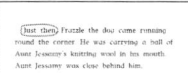

Text knowledge – relate familiar story themes to own experience

Talk about how Kate and Joe solved the problem of measuring their sunflower. Ask the children to suggest suitable tools to measure such objects in the classroom as a table, wall, book, bookshelf, floor and door.

Responding to the text

- Ask the children how Kate and Joe finally succeeded in measuring the sunflower.
- Can they explain why the other things they tried did not work?
- Can the children indicate the height of 2 metres and ten centimetres? Is this, for example, as high as a house or as a table?
- Has anyone ever grown a sunflower or entered a sunflower competition?

❶ Grow a sunflower

AIM to write simple instructions for planting a sunflower seed
(*NLS: Y2 T1 T15; S2*)

YOU WILL NEED
● sunflower seeds (or similar)

● soil

● small pots

● alternatively, you could use a book about growing sunflowers to demonstrate the process

WHAT TO DO Explain to the children that they are going to write simple instructions for planting and growing a sunflower (or other plant as appropriate). Work with them to plant some seeds in pots. Encourage them to talk about what they are doing as they plant their seeds, paying particular attention to the language used to explain a sequence of actions, e.g.

First you... (fill the pot with soil)
Then you... (place the seed below the surface)
Next you... (water it)
Then... (place it on the window ledge)

The children can write up and illustrate their instructions as a poster for display in the classroom. They can add further comments as the seeds begin to grow, e.g.

After a while... (a small shoot appears)

❷ Word Snap!

AIM to recognize the common spelling patterns for vowel phonemes *oo, ar, ow* (*NLS: Y2 T1 W3*)

YOU WILL NEED ● pieces of card (playing-card size) with words containing the above phonemes written on them, e.g.

wood / good / wool
mark / garden / far / park / bar / card / hard / jar / alarm / harm / farm / lark / dark / bark / car / yarn
wow / out / flower / about / down / clown / round / mound / pound / ground / found / crown / cow / how / now

WHAT TO DO Explain to the children that the object of the game is to play Snap by matching words containing the same vowel phoneme. The winner is the child with the most cards.

What's in the shed?

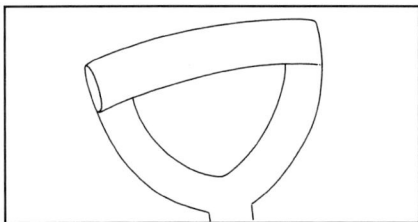

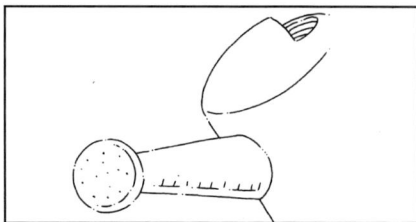

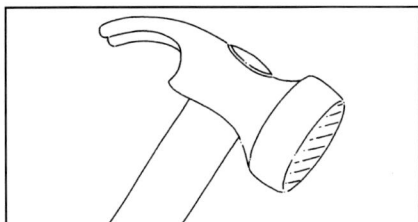

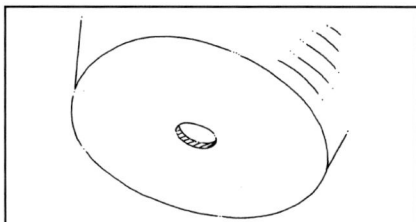

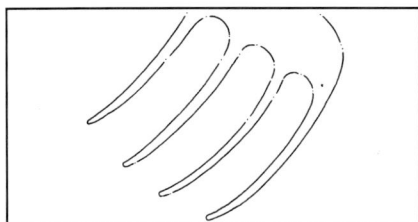

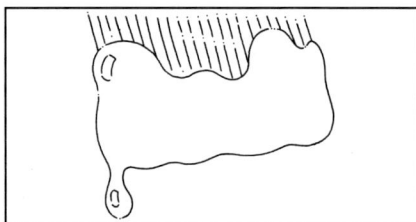

plant pot	paint	watering can	toy box
chair	spade	hammer	fork

Ask the children to identify the objects in the pictures above, and to write down what they are. They could check their spellings using a dictionary. They can then try to think of other objects that might be found in a garden shed. You may need to prompt them with ideas.

How Big Is It?   *(NLS: Y2 T1 W10)*